The Stop Smoking

Colouring Book for Self-Hypnosis

ESTHER PINCINI

The Stop Smoking Colouring Book for Self-Hypnosis
by Esther Pincini

Copyright © Magdalene Press 2018

ISBN 978-1-77335-108-7

No part of this publication may be reproduced, stored in a retrieval system, or transmitted in any form or by any means, electronic, mechanical, photocopying, recording or otherwise without written permission of the publisher.

Magdalene Press, 2018

Stopping smoking will make you

1. Smell better
2. Be Calmer
3. Have more money

4. Have whiter teeth and cleaner fingers

5. Stop coughing

6. Go places without

worrying about the next cigarette

7. Fit in

8. Have better skin and look healthier

9. Feel like a success

10. Stop playing Russian Roulette

You want to stop.

Smoking is disgusting.

You are a non-smoker.

You are a beautiful non-smoker.

Stopping smoking will make you

1. Smell better

2. Be Calmer

3. Have more money

4. Have whiter teeth and cleaner fingers

5. Stop coughing

6. Go places without

worrying about

the next

cigarette

7. Fit in

8. Have better skin and look healthier

9. Feel like a success

10. Stop playing Russian Roulette

You want to

stop.

Smoking is disgusting.

You are a non-smoker.

You are a beautiful non-smoker.

Stopping smoking will make you

1. Smell better
2. Be Calmer
3. Have more money

4. Have whiter teeth and cleaner fingers

5. Stop coughing

6. Go places without

worrying about

the next

cigarette

7. Fit in

8. Have better skin and look healthier

9. Feel like a success

10. Stop playing Russian Roulette

You want to stop.

Smoking is disgusting.

You are a non-smoker.

You are a beautiful non-smoker.

Stopping smoking will make you

1. Smell better
2. Be Calmer
3. Have more money

4. Have whiter teeth and cleaner fingers

5. Stop coughing

6. Go places without

worrying about the next cigarette

7. Fit in

8. Have better skin and look healthier

9. Feel like a success

10. Stop playing Russian Roulette

You want to stop.

Smoking is disgusting.

You are a non-smoker.

You are a beautiful non-smoker.

Stopping smoking will make you

1. Smell better
2. Be Calmer
3. Have more money

4. Have whiter teeth and cleaner fingers

5. Stop coughing

6. Go places without

worrying about

the next

cigarette

7. Fit in

8. Have better skin and look healthier

9. Feel like a success

10. Stop playing Russian Roulette

You want to stop.

Smoking is disgusting.

You are a non-smoker.

You are a beautiful non-smoker.

Stopping smoking will make you

1. Smell better

2. Be Calmer

3. Have more money

4. Have whiter teeth and cleaner fingers

5. Stop coughing

6. Go places without

worrying about the next cigarette

7. Fit in

8. Have better skin and look healthier

9. Feel like a success

10. Stop playing Russian Roulette

You want to

stop.

Smoking is disgusting.

You are a non-smoker.

You are a beautiful non-smoker.

Stopping

smoking will

make you

1. Smell better

2. Be Calmer

3. Have more money

4. Have whiter teeth and cleaner fingers

5. Stop coughing

6. Go places without

worrying about the next cigarette

7. Fit in

8. Have better skin and look healthier

9. Feel like a success

10. Stop playing Russian Roulette

You want to stop.

Smoking is disgusting.

You are a non-smoker.

You are a beautiful non-smoker.

Stopping smoking will make you

1. Smell better
2. Be Calmer
3. Have more money

4. Have whiter teeth and cleaner fingers

5. Stop coughing

6. Go places without

worrying about

the next

cigarette

7. Fit in

8. Have better skin and look healthier

9. Feel like a success

success

10. Stop playing Russian Roulette

You want to stop.

Smoking is disgusting.

You are a non-smoker.

You are a beautiful non-smoker.

Stopping smoking will make you

1. Smell better
2. Be Calmer
3. Have more money

4. Have whiter teeth and cleaner fingers

5. Stop coughing

6. Go places without

worrying about

the next

cigarette

7. Fit in

8. Have better skin and look healthier

9. Feel like a success

10. Stop playing Russian Roulette

You want to stop.

Smoking is disgusting.

You are a non-smoker.

You are a beautiful non-smoker.

Quitting smoking will make you

1. Smell better

2. Be Calmer

3. Have more money

4. Have whiter teeth and cleaner fingers

5. Stop coughing

6. Go places without

worrying about

the next

cigarette

7. Fit in

8. Have better skin and look healthier

9. Feel like a success

success

10. Stop playing Russian Roulette

You want to

stop.

Smoking is disgusting.

You are a non-smoker.

You are a beautiful non-smoker.

www.ingramcontent.com/pod-product-compliance
Lightning Source LLC
Chambersburg PA
CBHW051120110526
44589CB00026B/2986